Craft it up this Ramadan and Eid

Have fun creating over 40 recyclable
crafts into things you love

Zayneb Abdullatif
Photography by Sidqie Djunaedi

Acknowledgements

It is by the Mercy of Allah (swt) that He has giving me the ability to write this book. After months of hard work, this book is finally complete, Alhamdulillah.

To my stepdaughter Shaafazka, my nieces; Issra and Salma, my nephews; Hussein, Ahmed, Issa and Mohamed. You are the source of my inspiration and helping me turn my ideas into a reality!

My husband Sidqie, thank you for your endless support, love and beautiful photography (and especially for putting up with me these past months).

My family and friends, thank you for all the encouragement and true belief in what I do.

Special thanks goes out to Razeena, Hajar and Famiza.

Jazaakum Allahu Khairan!

Text copyright © 2015 Zayneb Abdullatif
Photography copyright © 2015 Sidqie Djunaedi

All rights reserved. No part of this publication may be reproduced, stored in a retrieval system or transmitted in any form or by any means, electronic, mechanical, photocopying, recording or otherwise, without the prior written permission of the copyright owner.

ISBN: 978-0-6485425-0-6

Dedicated to a bunch of cheeky children in my life:
Shaafazka, Hussein, Ahmed, Issra, Salma, Issa and Mohamed.
Your vivid imagination and ideas have inspired me to create this craft book.

Contents

Introduction	7
Tips for parents and guardians	8
How to use this book	8
Recycle and reuse	9
Craft tools	9
Handy extras	9
The basics	10
Recipe basics	10
Sewing basics	12
The joyous month	14
Framed activity calendar	16
Scrapbook activity calendar	18
Flourishing deeds tree	20
Good deed sticks	22
Dua holder	23
Qur'an holder	24
Doily bowls	25
Clay plate	26
Weaved basket	28
Felt bookmarks	30
Paperclip bookmarks	32
Moon garland	33
Play masjid	34
Little Mu'meens	35
No sew apron	36
Journal	38
Cookbook	40
Sadaqah box	41
Sideeka the sheep	42
Dua wall décor	44

Silhouette glass lamp 45

A special festival 46

Accordion pinwheel décor 48
Eid Mubarak garland 50
Message jars 51
Origami vase 52
Fabric flowers 54
Pom poms 56
Crepe roses 57
Money envelopes 58
Mini Cases 60
Gift pouches 61
Love heart décor 62
Dua frame 63
Plaque 64
Magnets 65
Surprise in the mailbox 66
Button card 67
Pop up card 68
Sparkling gift tags 70
Clay tags 70
Mini flowers 71
Glitter gift wrap 72
Twine stamps 72
Polka dot gift wrap 73
Stencil gift wrap 73
Stationary wrap 74
Pencil wrap 75

Templates 76
Good deeds activity list 78
Glossary 79

Introduction

Craft it up this Ramadan and Eid

Handmade projects – we love them! Learning along the way is a bonus! This book is about inspiring children's imaginations while having fun seeking Islamic knowledge.

Initially I was searching far and wide to find an Islamic craft book that instills Islamic values and traditions. After months of searching I had no luck. So it got me thinking; what if I can create one? So that's what happened.

As a child growing up with 9 other siblings, we were always taught not to waste things. I guess that's why recycling became second nature. Rule of thumb; if it was in the house we would use it.

I believe in using less and making the most of what I have. That's why most projects on the following pages are created from recyclable items; that are found in your very own home…or maybe your next door neighbours ^_^

There are no rules in this book. Experiment with colour, texture and items. Unleash your creativity and overall have fun!

Zayneb Abdullatif

Tips for Parents and Guardians

This book encourages parents and children to come together and get creative! Children will have fun crafting while learning about Islamic values and traditions.

This book is suitable for children aged 6 years +, although younger children can help with simple tasks like using scissors, applying glue to objects and drawing simple shapes.

How to use this book

Most crafts in this book can be made using different materials and techniques. I have made some projects twice using different materials to ease the level of difficulty for younger children. Children will be able to complete steps either on their own or with adult supervision.

Firstly, pick a craft, read the instructions together and gather the materials required. Don't worry if you don't have all materials; experiment with different items and tools. If the end result doesn't look like what's pictured, it's okay! It's all about children using their imagination and creating their unique individual style!

Children absorb information very well. That's why most crafts have a brief Islamic introduction or activity, which allows them to understand why they are creating this craft.

Throughout the book you will see these symbols:

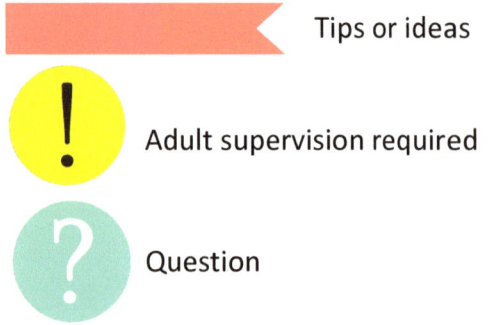

Tips or ideas

Adult supervision required

Question

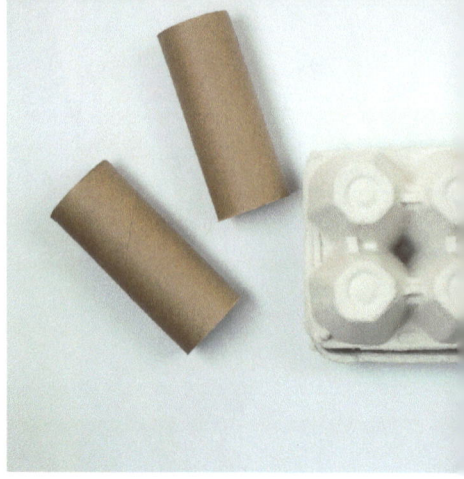

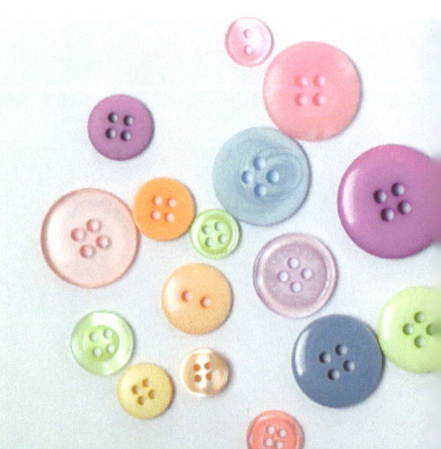

Recycle and reuse

As Muslims, we are taught to consider recycling and fixing before buying new things. Let's help save the Earth by collecting things we can reuse. Not only that, you'll also be saving which means more pocket money for you.

- Coloured paper
- Cardboard sheets & boxes
- Toilet rolls and egg cartons
- String, twine and ribbon
- Newspapers and magazines
- Wooden or plastic ice cream sticks
- Tissue paper
- Household objects; plastic containers, cans and jars
- Tree branches

Craft tools

This is a checklist to get you started.

- Scissors
- PVA glue and glue spreader
- Pencil
- Measuring tape
- Double sided tape
- Ruler
- Craft mat and craft knife
- Needle and thread
- Hot glue gun
- Mini hole punch

Handy extras

- Felt
- Ribbon
- Glitter and all sorts of embellishments

The basics

Recipe basics

Paper Mache Glue

Paper mache glue can be made from common household supplies. It's simple but can get a little messy, so be prepared!

Things you need:

- ½ cup of plain flour
- 4 cups of cold water
- 3 tablespoons of sugar
- Bowl
- Saucepan
- Wooden spoon

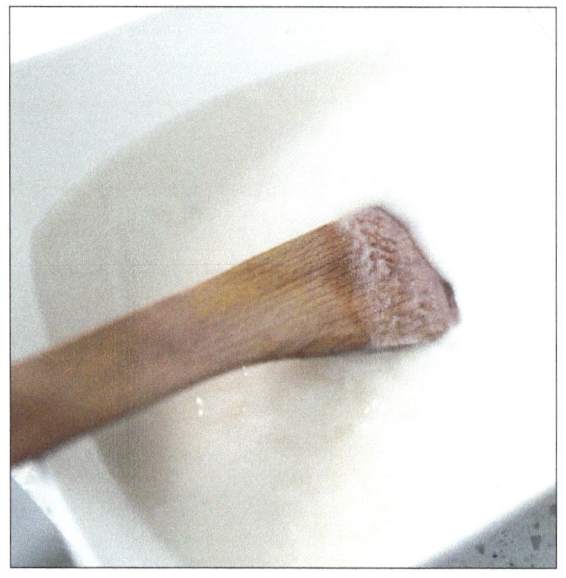

How to make:

1. Combine ½ cup of flour and 2 cups of cold water in a bowl and mix.

2. Boil 2 cups of water in a saucepan and add the flour and cold water mixture. Mix and bring to a boil.

3. Remove from heat and add 3 tablespoons of sugar. Let it cool. The paste will thicken as it cools.

Clay

Recipe basics

Making clay is easy and fun! Try this recipe to make some amazing crafts found in this book.

Things you need:

- 2 cups of baking soda
- 1 cup of cornflour
- 1 and a ½ cups of cold water
- Bowl
- Saucepan
- Wooden spoon

How to make:

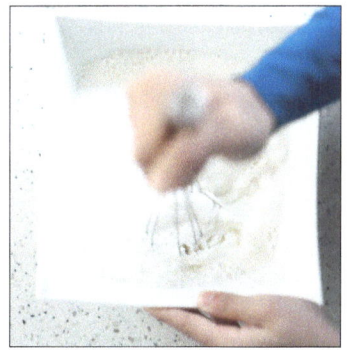

1. Mix all ingredients in a bowl together. Optional: if you would like to add food colouring, now is the best time to do so.

2. Add the mixture in a saucepan and cook over medium-high heat, stirring constantly. The mixture will begin to bubble and then clump together.

4. Transfer clay to a bowl and cover with a damp towel until cool. Once cool, knead until smooth. If clay is a little damp, add some cornflour.

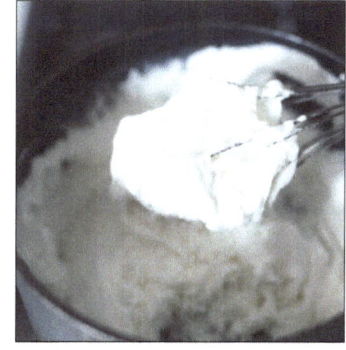

3. Keep mixing until the consistency is similar to mashed potato.

Store leftover clay for 1 month in a damp tea towel, sealing it inside a zip lock bag and refrigerating it

The basics
Sewing basics

These are just a few simple stitches used in this book. If you know of any others try experimenting with the craft projects.

Running stitch: This stitch is as simple as guiding your needle in and out through the fabric.

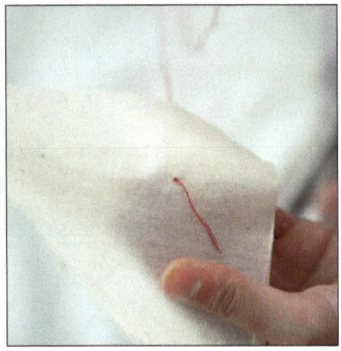

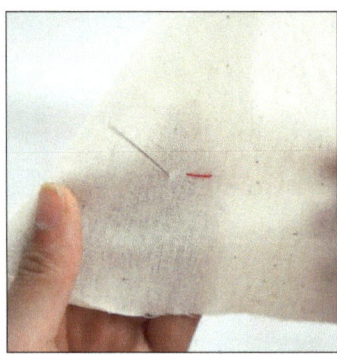

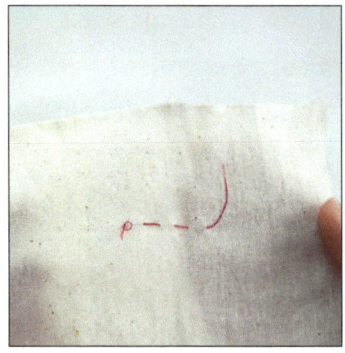

1. Thread the needle and knot the end.

2. Weave the needle in and out of the fabric creating the look of a dashed line.

3. Stitch about 0.5 cm stitches with equal length spaces between. Tie a knot at the end once finished.

Sewing basics

Blanket stitch: This is commonly used to edge a piece of fabric or outline a design.

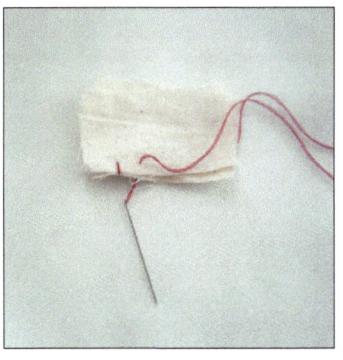

1. Thread the needle and tie a knot at the end. Start between the two layers and poke the needle down through the bottom layer.

2. Anchor the stitch by poking the needle down from the top layer (same position as last) making a loop. Poke the needle (sideways) through the loop and pull thread.

3. To start stitching, poke the needle down from the top.

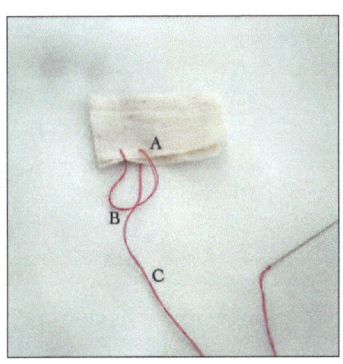

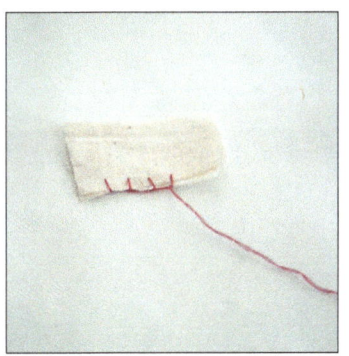

4. To complete the first stitch, bring the needle up from the back (A), and through the loop of thread (B). This should create a straight line down (C) before pulling the stitch tight.

5. Continue stitching until you reach the starting stitch. Then end the stitch by poking the needle through the bottom layer and tie the final knot.

The Joyous Month

Can you guess this joyous month?

- It is a special time for Muslims around the world
- During this time Muslims increase their worship to Allah (swt)
- Muslims must be on their best behaviour; being respectful, honest and helping others
- It appears once a year when the first silver of the crescent moon appears
- Allah (swt) has ordered Muslims to observe the fast in this month

Have you guessed it yet?
That's correct. It is the month of Ramadan, a special month for all Muslims, big and small.

Ramadan is a special gift from Allah (swt), so we can reconnect and get closer to Him through patience, prayers and Qur'an recitation. During this month, Muslims observe fasting with no food or drink from sunrise until sunset. Before sunrise, Muslims wake up and have suhoor. When the sun has set, it's time for iftar.

Ramadan is also about thinking of the less fortunate and how grateful we are to have countless blessings around us like water, food, clothing and shelter. It's a time for Muslims to be more kind and generous especially when giving their wealth away.
Are you looking forward to Ramadan?

1. Framed Activity Calendar

Upcycle any old frame into a Ramadan activity calendar. Now, the whole family can work together and help complete an activity a day. Have fun counting down this joyous month!

Things you need:

- Wooden frame (48 x 58 cm)
- 10 eye hooks
- 30 tiny pegs
- Sheets of double sided paper
- Twine
- Embellishments
- Markers
- Measuring tape
- Scissors

How to make:

1. Measure the inside edges of the frame and then divide and mark into 5 equal sections.

2. Fasten the eye screws on each marked section.

3. Attach twine from one end to the other.

To make the pouches;

4. Start with a 10 x 10 cm piece of double sided patterned paper & fold in half diagonally.

5. Take one of the corners and fold it over to the other side.

6. Do exactly the same to the other side.

7. Fold one of the upper corners down to secure the two folded corners.

8. Now begin to write Ramadan activities on small notes and insert into the pouches. If you're stuck on activities, turn to page 78 for a list of ideas.

Use a pushpin to make a small hole on the marked sections before inserting eye screw

2. Scrapbook Activity Calendar

Continue the fun and use your wildest imagination to come up with Islamic reminders, activities and even treats to add to your calendar. This is really fun so get your family involved too!

Things you need:

- 50 x 60 cm stiff cardboard
- Sheets of cardstock
- Embellishments
- Craft knife & mat
- Pencil
- Glue stick
- Ruler
- Scissors

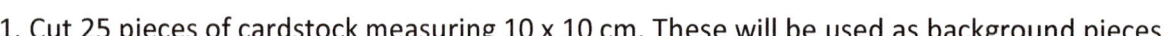

How to make:

1. Cut 25 pieces of cardstock measuring 10 x 10 cm. These will be used as background pieces.
2. Arrange your pieces on the cardboard. Don't glue just yet.

To make the opening flaps for the background pieces follow instructions below.

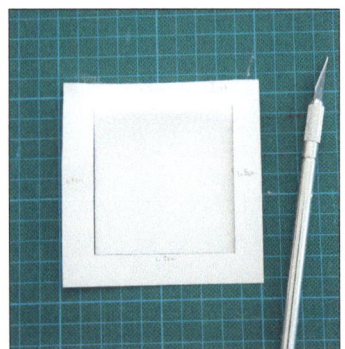

3. Take one background piece and mark 1.5 cm away from all edges.

4. Cut along these marked edges, leaving the topside uncut. The background piece should look like the above picture.

5. Make the pouches by following the activity on page 61. Then decorate, add numbers and then add daily activities (page 78).

3. Flourishing Deeds Tree

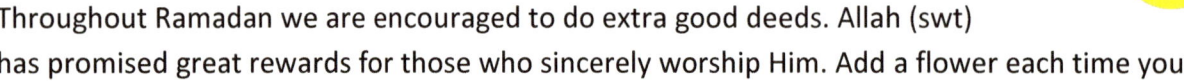

Throughout Ramadan we are encouraged to do extra good deeds. Allah (swt) has promised great rewards for those who sincerely worship Him. Add a flower each time you do a good deed and watch your tree blossom, just in time for Eid.

Things you need:

- Branches
- Sheets of patterned paper
- Large glass jar
- Pencil
- Double sided tape
- Hot glue gun
- Scissors

How to make:

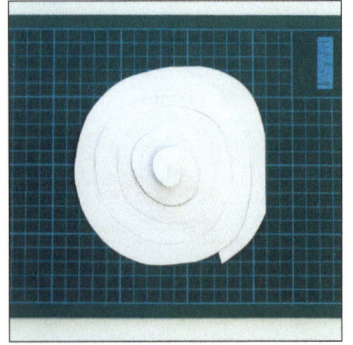

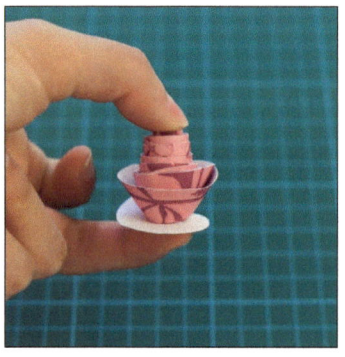

1. Draw a large spiral circle on a 15 x 15 cm piece of paper. Cut the spiral starting from the outside edge working your way to the middle. (The size of the paper will determine the size of your flower).

2. Start by rolling up the spiral from the outside all the way to the centre. Keep it as tight as you can. After rolling about 5 cm, add some tape to tighten the centre.

3. Stand your spiral upright and use the centre as a base. Begin to unravel. To create a bud, keep the unravelling process to a minimum and vice versa to create open blooms.

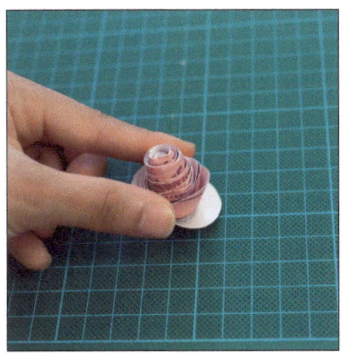  

4. Continue to unravel to create the width you prefer. Once you are happy with the way it looks, lift the upper-spiraled petals and add some glue to the base.

5. Lower the floral petals back down on the base and repeat the entire process for each good deed.

6. Place the branch in a decorated jar. Use the hot glue gun to stick flowers onto the branch each time a good deed has been completed.

> Cut wavy edges to add more character to your flower

4. Good Deed Sticks

Pick a stick and complete the task each day. We must remember do to good deeds to please Allah (swt) only. This means to do each good deed perfectly and with an honest heart.

Things you need:

- Fabric scraps
- Tin can or glass jar
- Embellishments
- Wooden skewers or ice cream sticks
- Patterned paper
- List of good deeds
- PVA glue
- Glue spreader
- Pen
- Scissors

How to make:

1. Decorate the tin or jar by gluing fabric and adding embellishments.
2. To make the flags, cut 30 (or more) shapes from the paper and then decorate.
3. Write down a good deed on each flag and then glue each flag to a stick.

> To stand the sticks upright, place some foam in the tin or jar

5. Dua holder

Do you sometimes forget the iftar dua? Make this dua holder so you can always remember what to say before you break your fast.

Things you need:

- Medium sized rock
- 60 cm of floral wire
- 1 paper clip
- Cardstock
- Pen
- Scissors

How to make:

1. Place rock in the middle of the wire leaving an equal amount of wire on each side.

2. Wind wire around the rock once, both vertically and horizontally.

3. Flip the rock over and twirl the remaining wire upright.

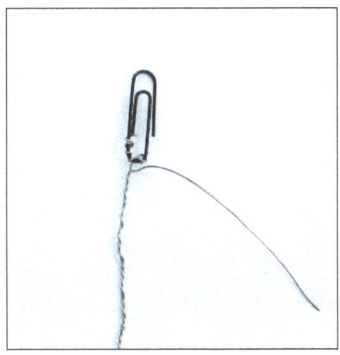

4. Leave 5 cm of wire at the end and twirl wire around the clip to hold it steady. Now write the dua on the cardstock.

Do you know what the iftar dua is? Turn to page 79 for some help.

6. Qur'an Holder

Ramadan is the month in which the Qur'an was sent down. It's important for us to recite and understand it as much as we can.

Things you need:

- Cereal or cardboard box
- Scrapbook paper
- Pencil
- PVA glue and glue spreader
- Ruler
- Scissors

How to make:

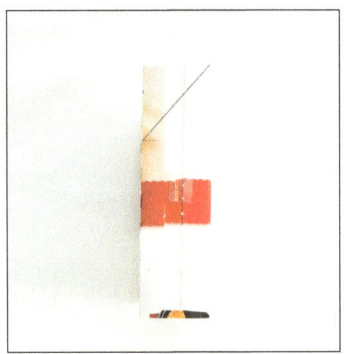

1. Draw a diagonal line on the narrow side, 12.5 cm away from the bottom.

2. Then draw a line directly across the main side.

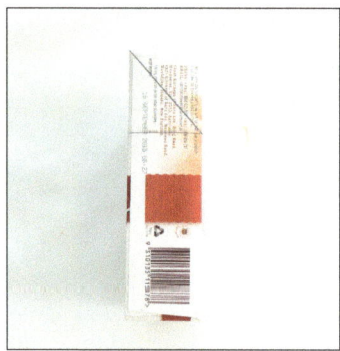

3. Continue to draw a diagonal line back on the opposite narrow side, 12.5 cm away from bottom.

4. Cut along the drawn lines leaving the back intact. Trace the paper according to the box size and cut. Glue paper on box and decorate.

7. Doily Bowls

Let's follow the sunnah of our beloved Prophet Muhammad (pbuh) by breaking our fast with dates. Get ready to make these beautiful gifts to distribute dates in for your family, friends and neighbours.

Things you need:

- Lace doilies
- ½ cup PVA glue
- Glue spreader or spoon
- Bowls
- ½ cup water
- Cling wrap

How to make:

1. Mix glue and water in a small bowl.

2. Soak doilies in the glue mixture and gently squeeze out excess solution.

3. Place cling wrap over bowls.

4. Place doilies over the bottom of the bowls and use your fingers to pat into place. Leave overnight to completely air dry and then remove doily and cling wrap from bowl.

Use a clean cloth to wipe down as doily will return to its original form if washed

8. Clay Plate

Dates are filled with important nutrients and energy to keep you healthy.
Say bismillah and enjoy the sweetness of these dates. Remember it's a sunnah to eat an odd number of dates.

Things you need:

- 1 quantity of clay
- Waxed paper
- Fabric doily or stamps
- Round object (to trace)
- Rolling pin
- Oven safe bowl
- Sand paper

How to make:

1. Prepare the clay (see page 11) and then preheat oven to 100 degrees.

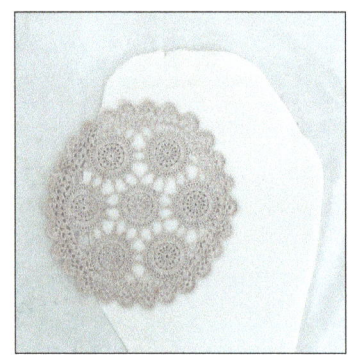

2. Roll out clay between two layers of waxed paper until it's 1-1.5 cm thick.

3. Place doily over clay and roll again. If you are using stamps, now is the time to stamp your design.

4. Remove doily slowly and position the round object firmly on the clay. Remove excess clay and save for future projects.

 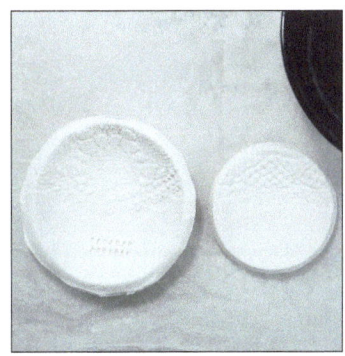 

5. Place clay into the bottom of the oven-safe bowl. Push it down a little so it takes the form of the bowl. Place the bowl into the oven for approx. 1 hour or until completely dry. Clay must be entirely cooked to avoid cracking.

6. Remove from oven and let it cool inside bowl for 20 minutes or so. When cool, turn the bowl over and it should pop right out.

7. Use sand paper to sand edges smooth.

> Use a chopstick or pencil to make holes to add twine or ribbon

9. Weaved basket

Giving a meal to a fasting person is very rewarding, even if you give just a date! You will even get the rewards of that fasting person too! Let's start weaving these beautiful paper baskets and hand some dates out!

Things you need:

- Plain paper
- Patterned paper
- Stapler
- Glue stick
- Paper clips
- Pegs
- Mini hole punch
- Twine
- Scissors

How to make:

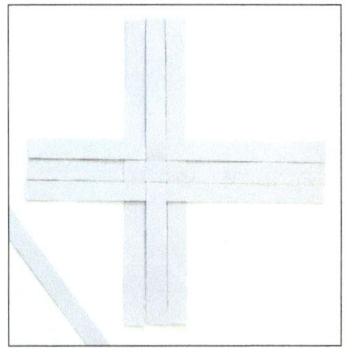

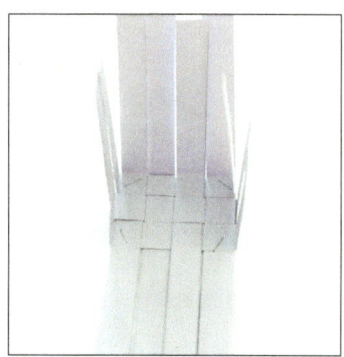

1. Cut 7 strips of plain paper 33 cm long and 2 cm wide. To form the base of the basket, lay 3 strips across 4 and weave together as shown above.

2. Use the stapler to staple each of the 4 corners to hold the base together.

3. Bend all the strips upwards to form a basket shape.

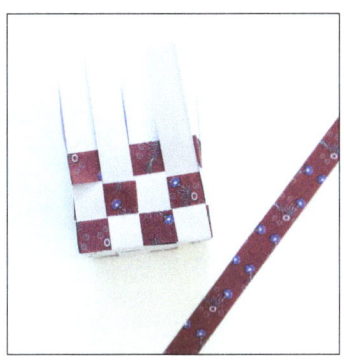  

4. Cut 3-4 strips of the patterned paper with previous measurements. Weave each strip over and under the plain strips. While weaving, gently bend the patterned strips at each corner to take the shape of the basket. Then glue the beginning and end of each patterned strip to keep it in place.

5. Continue weaving until all 3-4 patterned strips are in place then cut off the excess plain strips.

6. Cut a strip of plain paper 2.5 cm wide and long enough to go around the whole basket. Fold it in half (lengthways) and fit it over the rim. Place paper clips to temporarily hold in place.

This craft is best made with A3 paper

7. Use the hole punch to make holes on the rim. Thread twine through and over the rim. Once you reach the end, tie a double knot.

8. Cut a strip of plain paper 2.5 cm wide and 20 cm long. Cut the patterned paper 1.5 cm wide and 20 cm long and stick along the centre of the plain paper. Glue each end inside the basket and hold in place with pegs until handle is firmly attached.

10. Felt Bookmarks

We get extra rewards for every single letter we recite in Ramadan. Let's make these bookmarks to help encourage us to read and memorise the Qur'an.

Things you need:

- Felt- teal and beige coloured
- Round objects
- Ribbon
- Buttons
- Needle
- Cotton thread
- PVA glue
- Glue spreader
- Ruler
- Scissors

How to make:

We will be making the camel bookmark.

1. Trace round objects onto the felt to make 4 beige circles (bases) 4 cm in diameter, 1 teal circle 2.5 cm and another beige circle 1.5 cm. Cut a small camel from the teal felt.

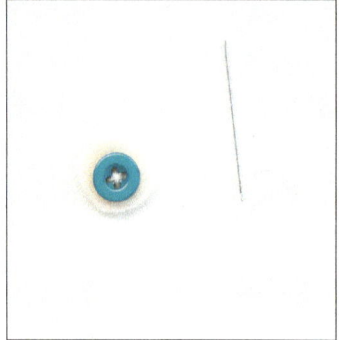

2. Thread the needle and knot the end. Stitch the teal button onto the small beige circle.

3. Now, stitch that small beige circle onto the teal circle using the running stitch method (page 12). If you like, alternate between the coloured thread.

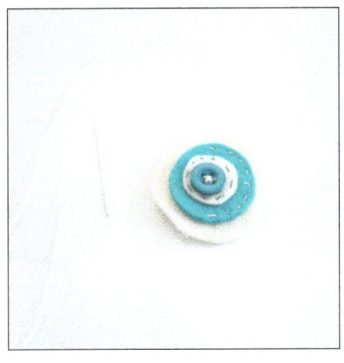

4. Stitch the same teal circle on one of the unused bases.

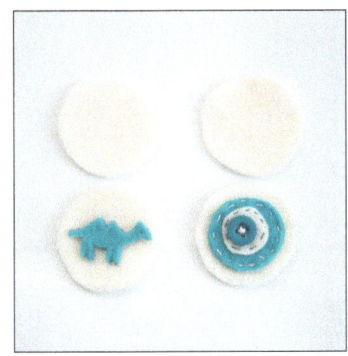

5. Pair up all bases together like above. Glue the camel on one of the beige bases.

6. Cut a 30 cm piece of ribbon.

7. Place the end of the ribbon in between one of the paired bases. Start stitching around the base using the blanket stitch method (page 13).

8. Keep stitching all the way to the end. Once you have reached the ribbon area, use the running stitch method (page 12).

9. Finish it off with a knot at the back. Now place the other end of the ribbon in between the other base and start stitching.

10. The camel base should look like the picture on the left.

If you don't have round objects with the correct measurements, make templates from paper

11. Paperclip Bookmarks

Encourage your family and friends to read the Qur'an with these super cute paperclip bookmarks. You will also get rewarded for your good deed. They're super easy to make too!

Things you need:

- Paperclips
- Thick cardstock
- Variety of buttons
- Embellishments
- Craft knife and mat
- Hot glue gun

How to make:

1. Use your imagination to create various designs from buttons.
2. Using the hot glue gun, stick buttons together and let it dry.
3. Turn the button around and add some glue on the back. Attach the paperclip.
4. Cut a rectangular shape from cardstock.
5. Decorate with a message and embellishments.
6. Use the craft knife to cut a small slit on the cardstock, just above the middle or wherever you prefer. Insert your bookmark.

Use felt or paper to also make paperclip bookmarks

What's your favourite surah in the Qur'an and why?

12. Moon Garland

Allah (swt) has made the moon as a sign and a way to measure the months and years. Make this craft to help you learn about the moon phases and then try to find them throughout Ramadan.

Things you need:

- Black and white cardstock
- Twine
- Round object (to trace)
- Pencil
- Tape
- Scissors

How to make:

1. On black cardstock, trace the round object to make 5 circles. Using white cardstock, draw all the moon phases (as shown).
2. Use black cardstock to draw 5 banners and on each banner write down the moon phases including: New Moon, Crescent, Half Moon, Gibbous and Full Moon.
3. Cut all shapes out, then glue the white moon phases on the black circles.
4. Cut a piece of twine measuring about 100 cm and tie a loop at the top (to hang).
5. Position the moon phases in order vertically and then tape them to the twine.
6. Hang the moon garland on the wall and place a white sheet besides it for extra notes.
   Optional: Tie a knot every 20 cm to even the positions of shapes.

13. Play Masjid

Use this play masjid as a beautiful display or head over to the next page and make the adorable little Mu'meens. After that, use your wildest imagination to think of a creative Ramadan story to present to family and friends. Are you ready? Thinking caps on!

Things you need:

- Stiff cardboard
- Pencil
- Sheets of scrapbook paper
- PVA glue
- Glue spreader
- Sharp knife

How to make:

1. Draw 2 mosques the same size on cardboard and cut out using a knife. If you like, you can also cut doors and windows.

2. On one mosque, cut one line starting from the bottom towards the centre. On the other, cut one line from the top until it reaches the centre.

3. Glue scrapbook paper on the mosques and slot together as shown on the main picture.

14. Little Mu'meens

These adorable Mu'meens will be perfect for your play masjid! Before you begin say bismillah!

Things you need:

- 1 Egg carton (makes 3-4 Mu'meens)
- Paint and brushes
- Bits of fabric
- Cotton balls
- PVA glue
- Glue spreader
- Scissors

How to make:

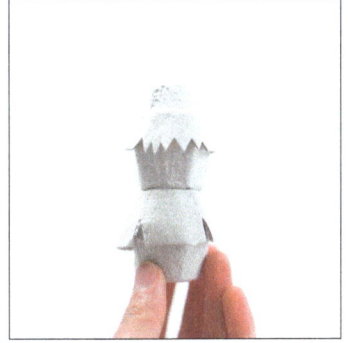

1. Cut 2 egg holders for the main body, (1 slightly smaller for the bottom half). Then cut another egg holder for the head. If you like, add a design to the top half egg holder by cutting some shapes out or anything you like.

2. Glue all pieces together, holding it for a minute or two until glue dries. Then cut out hair and a cap using the left over egg cartons and glue on as well.

3. Paint and decorate. For the females, add a cotton ball wrapped in fabric to give the head some shape (see page 55, step 4). Then cut some fabric and use as a hijab.

> The egg carton shape varies according to the manufacturer, adjust step 1 if needed

15. No Sew Apron

Let's gain extra good deeds and help our parents make iftar. Things can get real messy in the kitchen! It's time to make these aprons to stay clean!

Things you need:

- 1 metre fabric
- Tailors chalk
- 2 buttons (each with 4 button holes)
- No sew web tape
- Clothesline roping
- Iron
- Scissors

How to make:

1. Fold fabric in half and cut according to the template on page 76.

2. Unfold fabric and turn to the backside. Apply web tape along the bottom edge.

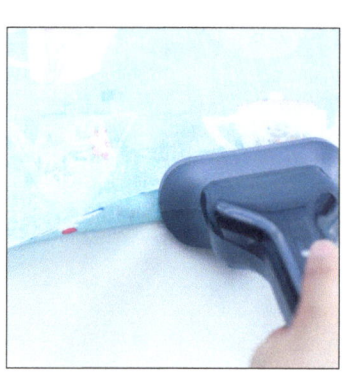

3. Now fold the bottom edge 2.5 cm over the web tape and iron. The tape will adhere to the fabric once ironed.

> Template measurements will fit older children between the ages of 10-13 years
> It's best to measure your child first

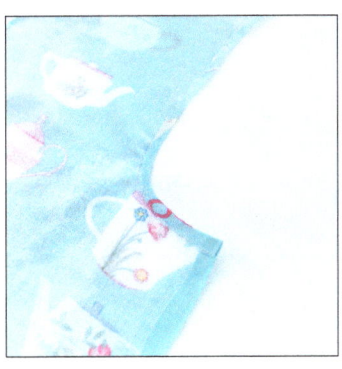

4. Repeat steps 2 and 3 on the left, right and curved sides.

5. Leave a 5 cm space at the top and fold. Directly beneath the edge of the fold, add a strip of web tape and iron. There should be a gap now.

6. Cut approx. 60 cm of rope to go around the neck. Feed the rope through the gap and tie a knot.

7. Cut 2 pieces of rope approx. 35 cm long. Now cut 2 small slits on the left side of the waistline.

8. Using a rope, feed 1 end through a hole. Then feed the other end diagonally through the other hole.

9. Repeat step 8 with the other piece of rope. Then feed the 2 ends of each rope through each separate slit.

10. Double knot. Repeat steps 7-10 on the other side.

11. Cut a pocket and apply web tape on the backside edges and then iron. Place web tape onto the apron where the pocket will be positioned and iron the pocket onto the apron. If you like, add some ribbon by using the web tape and iron.

16. Journal

Islam teaches us to share what we have learnt so that others may benefit and earn the blessings of Allah (swt). Let's make this journal to take extra notes in Ramadan, so that we can share with everyone around us.

Things you need:

- Bookbinding needle (blunt tip)
- Mini hole punch
- 70 cm of cotton yarn
- 30 sheets of white paper (12.5 x 17.5 cm)
- 2 decorative sheets (12.5 x 17.5 cm)
- Clip
- Ruler
- Scissors

How to make:

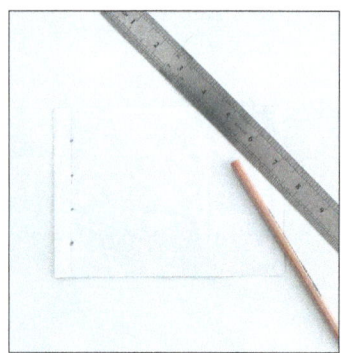

1. Use the back of 1 decorative sheet to mark 4 sewing positions 2.5 cm from the spine edge. Mark position 1 and 4 at least 2.5 cm from the top and bottom; positions 2 and 3 are equally spaced between.

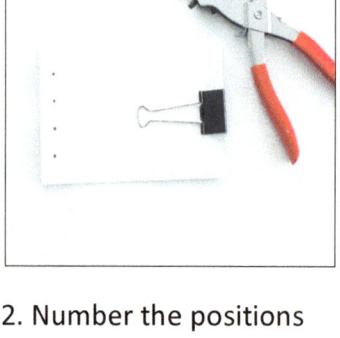

2. Number the positions in order from 1 to 4. Place all sheets together and use the clip to hold papers in place. Now hole punch the 4 markings.

3. Thread the needle and tie a knot at the end.

4. Begin at position 2 (back side facing you). Pull the needle through position 2 and pull tightly.

5. Wrap the needle around the spine edge and back through position 2. Then across, through position 1.

6. Wrap the needle around spine edge and back through position 1.

7. Wrap the needle around the top of the front cover and go through position 1.

8. Go through position 2. Go through position 3.

9. Go through position 4. Wrap the needle around the spine edge and back through position 4.

10. Wrap the needle around the bottom of the front cover and go through position 4.

11. Go through position 3. Wrap the needle around the spine edge and back through position 3.

12. Go through position 2 and tie a knot to secure.

17. Cookbook

Food plays a big role in celebrating Ramadan. We must remember not to waste food because the food thrown away can be someone else's meal. Let's plan ahead with these cookbooks!

Things you need:

- 8-10 brown paper bags (same size)
- Cardstock
- Pencil
- Embellishments
- Hole punch
- Ribbon
- Glue
- Scissors

How to make:

1. Stack bags on top of each other, alternating open and closed ends.

2. Fold the bags in half making a sharp crease.

4. Bind the book with ribbon and decorate the front cover. Use the 'opening pockets' to insert pictures or extra recipe cards.

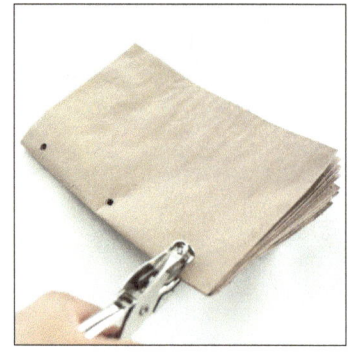

3. Mark 3 circles along the spine of the bags and then hole punch. If bags are too thick, separate them, punching 2 bags at a time. Ensure all holes are in the same position.

18. Sadaqah Box

Make sadaqah a regular habit especially in Ramadan. Once you figured out where you want your sadaqah to be donated, encourage family members to do the same. Together, your small donations can help many people!

Things you need:

- Shadow box
- Scrapbook paper
- Embellishments
- Glue stick
- Sharp knife
- Scissors

How to make:

1. Decorate the base of the box with scrapbook paper and embellishments. It's a good idea to decorate the base with pictures of where you want your sadaqah to be donated.
2. Optional: decorate the outside of box.
3. Cut a slot area to insert money at the top with a knife.

If the box is too thick and you're having difficulty cutting through, try cutting a slot at the back of the base to insert money.

Why is it so important to give money to the less fortunate or help those in need?

41

19. Sideeka the Sheep

As Muslims we have an obligation to help those less fortunate. Allah (swt) has told us in the Qur'an that our wealth will be blessed and doubled when we give in charity.

Things you need:

- Balloon
- Newspaper
- Egg carton
- Cotton balls (heaps)
- Paper mache glue
- PVA glue
- Glue spreader
- Sharp knife
- Paint
- Paintbrushes

How to make:

1. Prepare 1 quantity of paper mache glue (see page 10) and then blow up the balloon.

2. Tear newspaper into 3 cm wide strips and apply with paper mache glue onto the balloon, smoothing as you go.

3. Repeat until you've built up 4-6 layers all over. The more layers the better. Leave in an airy place for a couple of days until the newspaper is bone dry.

4. Dip sheets of newspaper into the paper mache glue and form the shapes of ears, a face and a tail. Place them with the balloon so they can be completely bone dry.

5. Once dry, take the knife and carefully cut a slot for the money to go in. The balloon will pop and you can pull it out from the hole you just made.

6. Cut 4 egg holders to use as feet. Cut the front feet a little bigger and the back feet slightly smaller and curvier so the weight is balanced. Stick with PVA glue at the bottom of the balloon.

7. Glue on the face, ears and tail using PVA glue.

8. Cover the top half with PVA glue and stick the cotton balls on. Then paint the face, ears, feet and the rest of the body.

If you want to cut an opening slot underneath to remove money, cut it during step 5

Is sadaqah only limited to giving money away? What are other ways of giving sadaqah?

20. Dua Wall Décor

Something hanging on your wall can be a constant reminder to yourself and others. Create this fantastic wall décor and fill it with daily reminders and dhikr.

Things you need:

- Shoebox lids (assorted sizes)
- Scrapbook paper
- Embellishments
- Pegs
- PVA glue
- Glue spreader
- Tape
- Ribbon
- Scissors

How to make:

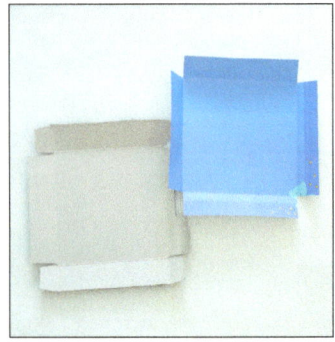

1. Flatten the shoebox lids, then trace them onto paper and cut out.

2. Glue the paper inside the lids and bring the sides back up to normal position (use tape to hold in place). Position the lids in the layout you want and decorate with some Ramadan reminders and pictures. Try not to add heavy embellishments, as this will be hung up.

3. Use PVA glue to stick the lid sides together. Use pegs to hold the lids in place. Once dry, attach some ribbon at the back.

21. Silhouette Glass Lamp

This can be displayed anywhere around the home. It's great for Ramadan gatherings or during dinner time.

Things you need:

- Empty glass jar
- Dark coloured paper
- Lace ribbon
- Pencil
- Craft knife and mat
- Measuring tape
- Double sided tape
- Tea light candle

How to make:

1. Start by measuring the circumference of your jar. This jar is 25 cm.
2. Determine how high you would like your silhouette picture to be.
3. Outline the measurements on the cardstock and start sketching your picture.
4. Cut out the silhouette using the craft knife. Allow an extra 1 cm at the end for a tab.
5. Wrap the silhouette around the outside of the jar and use tape to stick the two ends together. Optional: add tape on the backside of the silhouette before wrapping onto the jar.
6. Tie a ribbon at the top and add a nice scented tea light candle inside.

Add some twine thread around the top and hang outside during those long summer nights

A month of fasting and spiritual reflection has passed and we welcome a new celebration, Eid al Fitr.

Before the sun rises, Muslims prepare themselves by washing up and putting their best clothing on. They head towards the masjid to offer prayers. Before the Eid prayer, Muslims must offer a special charity called Zakat al Fitr. This is then distributed amongst the poor so they too can celebrate.

After the Eid prayer, the beautiful chanting of Takbirs can be heard -
"God is great, there is none worthy of worship but God; God is great, Praise be to Him."

Eid is a special time for visits and gatherings amongst family, friends and the community. Greetings are passed on to one another. Special foods and sweets are prepared. Children and adults exchange gifts and money. It's a special time where new friends are made and families spend quality time together.

While many Muslims don't have lavish Eids, we should be grateful for Allah's (swt) blessings and should open our hearts and share with others.

Another special festival is Eid al Adha. This Eid is to remember the trials of Prophet Ibrahim (as). Muslims all over the world slaughter an animal such as a sheep, cow or goat. One third of the meat sacrificed is eaten by family and relatives, one third is given away to friends and neighbours and one third is distributed to the poor.

This special act signifies our willingness to help others in need and give up things close to our hearts in order to follow Allah's (swt) commands.

22. Accordion Pinwheel Décor

Eid is around the corner, have you prepared? Let's celebrate the completion of good deeds by decorating our homes. It's heaps of fun! Invite your family and friends to give you a hand.

Things you need:

- 30 x 30 cm scrapbook paper
- Buttons
- Kraft paper
- Hot glue gun
- Ruler
- Pencil
- Scissors

How to make:

1. Each pinwheel needs 2 strips of paper. Measure and cut long strips of paper with a width of about 7-10 cm.

2. Evenly fold the 2 strips of paper in accordion style; fold the paper horizontally making a sharp crease and then fold in the opposite direction, then repeat. The pattern will be more visible if the folds are wider.

3. Take one strip; bend the accordion so that it is sitting in a half-circle. Then add a dab of glue to the bottom centre so the paper can hold its shape. Repeat with the other strip.

4. Once dry, add some glue to one of the bottom folds on the half circle.

5. Then stick two half circles together, and hold firm until glue is dry. It should look like the above picture.

6. Repeat steps 4-5 on the other side. Cut circle shapes from kraft paper big enough to cover the centre of each pinwheel. Glue a button on each circle, then glue the circles on the pinwheel (as shown below).

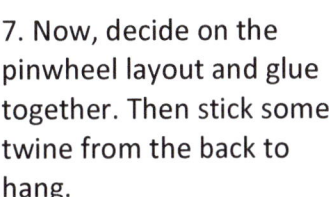

7. Now, decide on the pinwheel layout and glue together. Then stick some twine from the back to hang.

String the pinwheel vertically, in rows or from a stick for an Eid photo booth backdrop!

23. Eid Mubarak Garland

If you want to keep things nice and simple, this paper garland is perfect! You can even turn old book pages into one of these!

Things you need:

- Patterned paper
- Round object (6 cm diameter)
- Pencil
- 3.5 metres of twine
- PVA glue
- Glue spreader
- Mini hole punch
- Scissors

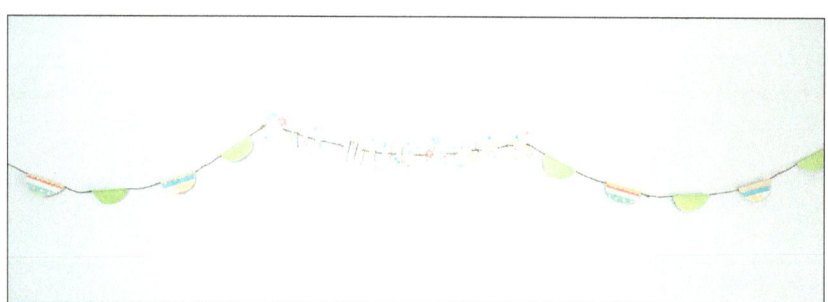

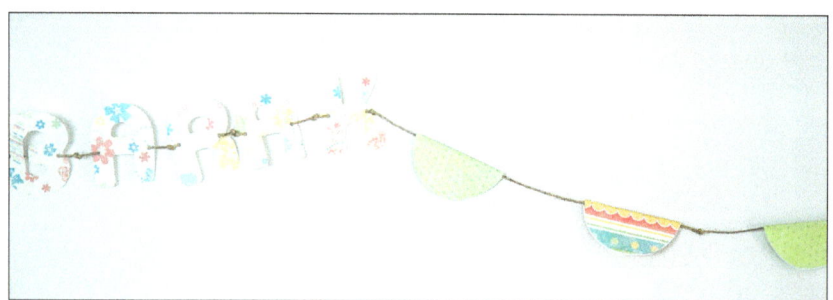

How to make:

1. Trace the round object to make 14 circles on paper and then cut out.
2. Make a sharp crease by folding circles in half with blank sides together.
3. Draw 'Eid Mubarak' letters and cut out. Punch small holes on both left and right sides of each letter.
4. Leave approx. 65-70 cm of twine at the beginning and end to hang garland.
5. Begin with 7 circles and place them 5 cm apart with twine in between folds.
6. Spread glue on the blank side of each circle and fold both sides together with twine directly on the centre crease.
7. Once all 7 circles are attached, leave a 5 cm gap then tie a knot. Now feed twine through each letter, tying a knot in between the letters (to hold in place). Once letters are attached, leave a 5 cm gap and repeat steps 5-6.

24. Message Jars

Make these funky message jars and fill it up with colourful flowers the night before Eid. I'm sure it will brighten up the room and create a warm and welcoming atmosphere.

Things you need:

- Hot glue gun
- Clean glass jar
- White matte spray paint
- Twine

How to make:

1. Turn on the hot glue gun and wait until it becomes hot.
2. Start writing on the jar. Be careful you don't touch the hot glue.
3. Wait until glue is dry then spray paint the outer side of the jar.
4. Leave to dry for approx. 5-10 minutes, then repeat the spray until it's completely covered.
5. Decorate by adding some twine around the jar. The roses pictured can be found on page 57.

Be sure to have a facemask on and spray in the backyard!

25. Origami Vase

Sometimes the simplest things can make someone smile, and smiling is a sunnah. Make this paper vase with flowers and gift it to a loved one. There's heaps of folding but it's great fun!

Things you need:

- 30 x 30 cm paper
- Ruler or bone folder
- Double sided tape
- Glass jar

How to make:

1. Fold paper in half and crease the middle using a ruler. Flip paper over and repeat on the other side.

2. Open the paper up and fold one edge into the middle to meet the new crease you just made. Repeat on the other side. The paper should be divided into four even sections now.

3. Fold the first of your fold sections in half again by taking one edge and folding it to meet the first fold. Then repeat with the other three sections.

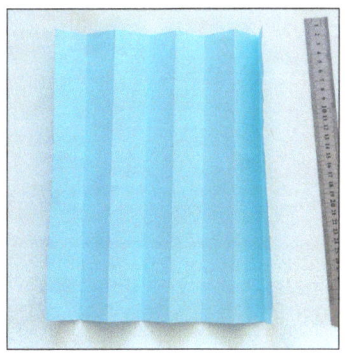

4. The paper should be divided into eight even sections now.

5. To make the diagonal folds, take the first corner and fold it to meet the first fold. It should form a right-angled triangle.

6. Take the same corner and fold it to meet the third vertical fold.

7. Take the same corner and fold it to meet the fifth vertical fold.

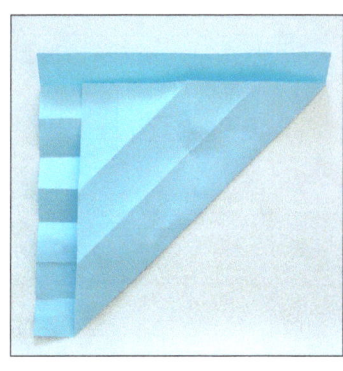

8. Take the same corner and fold it to meet the seventh vertical fold. Repeat steps 4-8 until all four corners are complete.

9. Gently curl your paper. The vase should start to form now. Add double sided tape on the inside spine and stick together.

10. Slide your vase over a glass jar and add a few branches. Create the flower craft on page 71 and glue onto branches. Now your vase is complete.

Use patterned paper to create a beautiful decorative vase.

26. Fabric Flowers

Allah (swt) has told us in the Qur'an not waste things. Try recycling old clothing or sheets to make these wonderful fabric flowers.

Things you need:

- 80 x 80 cm of fabric
- Paper
- 4-6 cotton balls
- Needle
- 35-40 cm of thread
- Hot glue gun
- Scissors

How to make:

1. Make a template by cutting a 10 cm circle from paper. Use this template to cut another circle from fabric.

2. Insert thread through needle and knot the ends. Stitch the edges of the circle using the running stitch method (page 12).

3. Once finished, pull the thread to create a ruffled look.

4. Insert cotton balls inside the fabric and close by pulling the thread and tying a knot in the final stitch. This will form the base.

5. Cut 5 strips of fabric, roughly 12 cm x 75 cm. This will make 2 fabric flowers. If you want to make one fabric flower, cut 3 strips.

6. Fold one strip of fabric in the middle, then fold again and again. This will make 8 circles, which will be your petals.

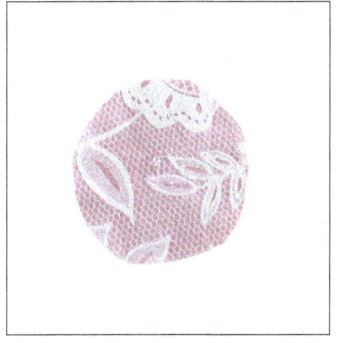

7. Trace the template on the folded fabric and cut. Repeat step 6-7 until you have about 40 petals.

8. Apply glue to the centre of the petal, fold in half and hold for 5 seconds.

9. Apply glue to the bottom centre and fold. Hold for 5 seconds and repeat with other circles.

10. Apply glue to the bottom of the petal and glue to the base.

11. Repeat steps 8-10 until base is covered. Then trim the edges for a neat look.

12. Optional: cut a small slit on the base and tie a ribbon for it to hang.

27. Pom Poms

Make these pom poms to decorate your house. It's a great way to brighten up the room. Recite some dhikr throughout this craft as it will earn you extra good deeds.

Things you need:

- 10 sheets of tissue paper
- Floral wire
- Ruler
- Scissors

How to make:

1. Stack 10 sheets of paper together, then measure 14 x 25 cm and cut.

2. Make 4 cm wide accordion folds, creasing with each fold (see page 48, step 2 for the accordion style fold).

3. Cut a small piece of floral wire. Place the wire around the centre of the paper and twist. With scissors, trim ends of paper into pointy shapes.

4. Separate layers by pulling away from the center one layer at a time. Repeat until all layers have been separated.

28. Crepe Roses

The simplest things can change someone's day. These roses are really quick and simple to make.

Things you need:

- Crepe paper
- 22 cm floral wire
- Pencils
- Tape
- Scissors

How to make:

1. Cut 60 cm of crepe paper.

2. Fold crepe paper every 4 cm until the whole strip is folded.

3. Cut a curve at the top.

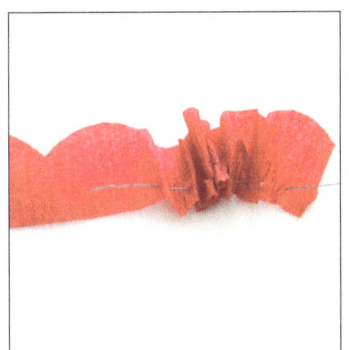

4. Unroll and then feed the wire into the crepe paper, gathering it until you reach the end.

5. Wrap the end of the wire around the pencil. Keep the crepe gathered to make it bloom.

6. Hold the pencil upright and start wrapping green crepe paper around to cover the pencil.

29. Money Envelopes

Giving gifts is one of the acts that Prophet Muhammad (pbuh) recommended. It maintains, strengthens and increases the love between the giver and the receiver.

Things you need:

- Cardstock
- 1 sheet of felt
- Tailors chalk
- Needle and thread
- 20-30 cm of cotton yarn
- 2 buttons
- Embellishments
- Ruler
- Pencil
- Scissors

How to make:

1. Trace template (page 76) on cardstock and cut out.

2. Use tailors chalk to transfer this template onto the felt sheet and cut out.

3. Bring the right hand side layer towards the left flap and pin together. Be careful not to pin the front layer as well.

4. Thread the needle with yarn and tie a knot at the end. Use the running stitch method (page 12) to stitch the pinned section from the bottom going upwards. Once finished tie a knot and cut the yarn.

5. Pin the bottom flap upward and start stitching right to left. Once finished, tie a knot and cut the yarn. If there are visible side knots, tuck them in.

6. The top flap should be the only side left untouched. Fold the flap down and estimate where the 2 buttons will be placed.

7. Use thread to stitch the bottom button and tie a knot. Then stitch the top button. Tie a knot and leave approx. 3-10 cm of thread then cut.

8. Cut cardstock slightly smaller than the envelope size and place inside. This is to keep the envelope firm.

9. Close the envelope by looping the thread around the bottom button, then around the top button. Keep repeating until a small amount of thread is left. Finish it off by adding embellishments.

> If you want to stitch any embellishments on the front, stitch it before commencing step 4

30. Mini Cases

A quick way to make a gift with hidden surprises! I'm sure any child would love this! Remember, it's always better to give than to receive.

Things you need:

- Toilet roll
- Patterned paper
- Ribbon
- Sweets and balloons
- Scissors

How to make:

1. Measure the circumference of the roll using the paper.

2. Cut and glue paper onto toilet roll.

3. Starting with the right side, push the end inwards.

4. Now the right side should look like this.

5. Fill with sweets. Then repeat step 3 on the left side and add ribbon.

31. Gift Pouches

Everyone loves gifts, especially younger children. These are simple gift pouches, which you can make and fill up with anything you like. Spread the joy of Eid around!

Things you need:

- Cardstock
- Pencil
- Sweets
- Hole punch
- Cellophane bag
- Twine
- Scissors

How to make:

1. On cardstock, draw the gift pouch template on page 76.

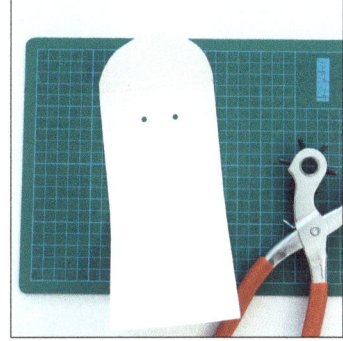

2. Cut and fold along the dotted lines. Use the hole punch to make 2 holes where marked.

3. Insert twine through the back of the cardstock. Place sweets in the cellophane bag and tie the bag.

4. Seal with a flower, some twine or anything you like.

32. Love Heart Décor

Trying hard to think of a gift but having no luck? Try making this beautiful heart made from egg cartons. You'll be helping the environment and saving money too!

Things you need:

- 1 egg carton
- 30 x 37 cm stiff cardboard
- Ribbon
- PVA glue
- Glue spreader
- Hole punch
- Paint and paint brush
- Scissors

How to make:

1. Cut the bottoms of the egg carton, about 3-4 cm of each egg holder, (ensure egg holders are the same size otherwise it will be difficult to glue them). Then paint each one.

2. From the top centre of the cardboard, mark and punch 2 holes, 10 cm apart. Then paint the cardboard.

3. Place egg holders in a heart shape on the cardboard and glue one by one. Once dry, paint the cardboard in between each egg holder. Decorate and thread ribbon to hang.

33. Dua Frame

Why not turn something old into something new! Recycle toilet rolls into this gorgeous frame and gift it to your teacher. Add a special dua to help say thank you for all their hard work.

Things you need:

- 8 empty toilet rolls
- Scrapbook paper
- PVA glue
- Glue spreader
- Paint
- Pegs
- Ruler
- Scissors

How to make:

1. Begin by slightly flattening your rolls. Mark each roll and cut into 2 cm pieces. You should have 5 pieces per roll.

2. Spread glue on one end of each piece and stick to another corner, holding firm with a peg. Repeat until you form a group of 4.

3. Place all rolls into a circle shape and glue only where the ends are touching. Hold firm with pegs and let it dry.

4. Paint and let it dry once more. Make the spiral flowers on page 20 and glue them onto frame. Finish this off by inserting a dua print and then glue white paper to cover the backing.

34. Plaque

The Prophet (pbuh) said, "Exchange gifts, as that will lead to increasing your love to one another." (Bukhari)

Things you need:

- 1 quantity of clay
- Wooden square
- Cookie cutters
- Stamps
- 2 eye screws
- Twine
- Embellishments
- Scissors

How to make:

1. Make clay (see page 11) then preheat oven to 100 degrees.

2. Roll out clay about 2.5 cm thick, stamp your design and then cut into shapes.

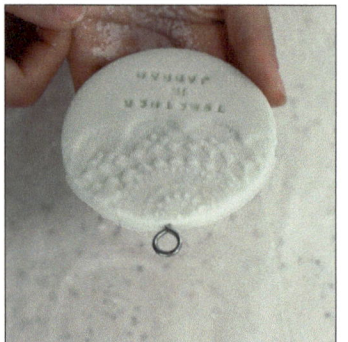

3. Insert the eye screw at the top of clay. Place on a tray and into the oven for an hour or so.

4. Meanwhile, decorate the wooden frame and insert an eye screen in the centre of the frame (from the inside).

5. Once cooked, let clay cool down, then attach twine through both eye screws and tie a bow.

35. Magnets

Always remember to gift something you would like to receive. If someone does give you a gift, you should respond by saying; 'Jazaak Allahu khairan'.
It simply means 'May Allah (swt) reward you with good'.

Things you need:

- 1 quantity of clay
- Rolling pin
- Stamps
- Cookie cutters
- Adhesive magnets
- Sandpaper

How to make:

1. Make clay (see page 11) then preheat oven to 100 degrees.

2. Roll out clay about 0.5-1 cm thick and stamp your design.

3. Punch out the shape of your magnets using a cookie cutter. Place in the oven for an hour or so. Set aside and dry overnight.

4. Once dry, sand any rough edges with sandpaper. If you like, decorate with paint.

5. Stick magnets on the back.

Clay should be thick when rolling, as this prevents cracking and becoming brittle when dry

36. Surprise in the Mailbox

If you live a mile away from loved ones, here's a great way to send something personal. They will definitely be blown away!

Things you need:

- Balloon
- Cardstock
- Pens
- Clip or peg
- Envelope
- Postage stamp

How to make:

1. Blow up the balloon and use the clip to stop it from deflating.

2. Write a special message to a loved one.

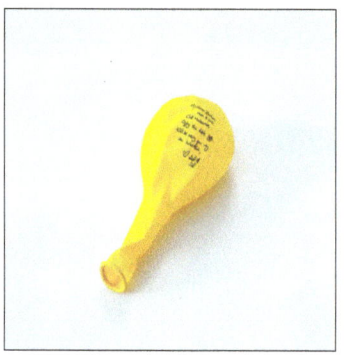

3. Once dried, deflate and decorate the cardstock. Then stick the balloon in the corner.

> Place a small picture of yourself in the balloon before sending

37. Button Cards

It takes some time to create a special gift for someone you love. Finish it off by adding a beautiful message inside like,
'I love for the sake of Allah (swt)'.

Things you need:

- Cardstock
- Assorted buttons
- Marker
- PVA glue
- Glue spreader
- Scissors

How to make:

1. Cut cardstock according to your desired card size. This card measures 12 x 23 cm. Fold in half.
2. On the front side, place buttons in the shape of a sheep's body. Don't glue just yet.
3. Draw the sheep head and legs with a marker.
4. Glue the buttons one by one carefully in their location.
5. Add a greeting or anything you like at the front and then write your message inside.

38. Pop Up Cards

Ideal for any occasion especially Eid! Make a personal pop up card for a loved one with your personalised message.

Things you need:

- Cardstock
- Embellishments
- Pencil
- Ruler
- Scissors

How to make:

1. Measure the card and fold in half. When folded this card measures 10 x 15.5 cm.

2. From the spine of the card draw 2 pairs of parallel lines of the same length. These parallel lines are 3 cm away from the top and bottom edges and equally divided in the middle.

3. Cut along the lines making sure you do not exceed cutting more than half of the card length, otherwise crafting bits will stick out when closed.

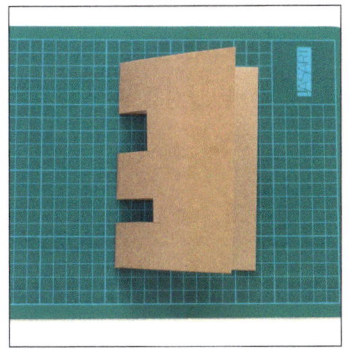 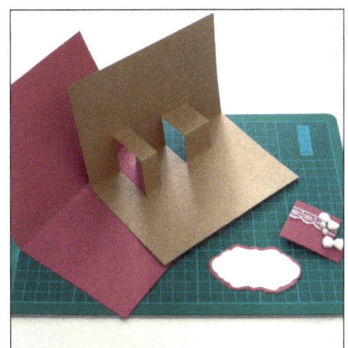 

4. Push the flaps forward. The card should look like this now.

5. Push the flaps forward and fold. Measure and cut another coloured cardstock just slightly bigger than the card (this will be the backing). Then start crafting your pieces to go inside card.

6. Glue the card on the outer cardstock and then glue the crafting pieces on the front part of the folded flaps (not the top).

39. Sparkling Gift Tags

If you don't have enough time to make a card, these gift tags will be perfect!

Things you need:

- Kraft cardstock
- Glitter
- Twine
- Pencil
- PVA glue
- Glue spreader
- Hole punch
- Scissors

How to make:

1. Draw a gift tag on cardstock and cut.
2. Spread PVA glue on the bottom half and place tag in a container (to avoid mess with glitter). Sprinkle glitter all over and shake excess glitter off.
3. Once dry, punch a small hole at the top and thread some twine through.

40. Clay Tags

Things you need:

- 1 quantity of clay
- Cookie cutters
- Stamps
- Pencil or Chopstick
- Twine
- Scissors

How to make:

1. Make clay (see page 11) and preheat oven to 100 degrees. Roll out clay about 1 -1.5 cm thick. Then stamp your design and cut into shapes.
2. Use the pencil to create a hole at the top. Place in the oven for an hour or so. Once dry, let it cool then if you like, decorate. Finish it off by threading twine through the hole.

41. Mini Flowers

Putting extra effort in little things can be very rewarding. Allah (swt) will reward us for every little good deed that we do purely for his sake only.

Things you need:
- Tissue Paper
- Marker
- Stapler
- Scissors

How to make:

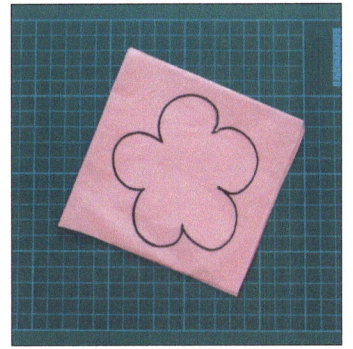

1. Lay 5 tissue papers over each other and draw a flower. The size of the drawing will determine the size of the flower.

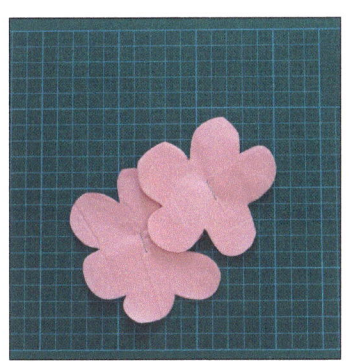

2. Staple the centre of the flower and cut.

3. Start by bringing the top layer up towards the centre and squishe so the petals remain upright.

4. Continue with all other layers leaving the last one unsquished.

42. Glitter Gift Wrap

Create your own personalised wrapping paper! Here are a few ideas but you can really experiment with anything at home like cookie cutters or toilet rolls!

Things you need:

- Kraft paper
- Double sided tape
- Glitter

How to make:

1. Cut paper and wrap the gift.
2. Stick double sided tape on the paper in any design you like.
3. Sprinkle glitter on the tape and shake off excess glitter. It's best to have a container underneath to avoid a big mess!

> Use washy tape instead

43. Twine Stamps

Things you need:

- Paper
- Thick cardboard
- Twine or hemp cord
- PVA glue
- Glue spreader
- Ink or paint

How to make:

1. Cut cardboard into a square or rectangle shape.
2. Draw your design on the cardboard.
3. Apply glue to the base of cardboard and then stick the twine according to your design.
4. Once dry, place ink or paint on twine and start stamping.

44. Polka Dot Gift Wrap

Things you need:

- Kraft paper
- Pencil
- Paint

How to make:

1. Using the end of the pencil, dip it into the paint then apply onto paper.
2. Repeat steps until your paper is covered with dots.
3. Once dry, wrap the gifts.

45. Stencil Gift Wrap

Things you need:

- Stencil
- Paper
- Paint
- Paint roller or sponge
- Sticky tape

How to make:

1. Tape the stencil on the paper.
2. Apply paint to roller or sponge and roll onto stencil.
3. Remove stencil. Once dry, wrap the gifts.

46. Stationary Wrap

The perfect gift for an artist or a writer! Jot down notes on the go and always remember to share what you know, so that others may also benefit.

Things you need:

- 21 x 29.7 cm (A4) felt sheet
- 60 -70 cm of ribbon
- 8 pencils
- Paper pad
- Craft knife and mat
- Ruler
- Tailor's Chalk

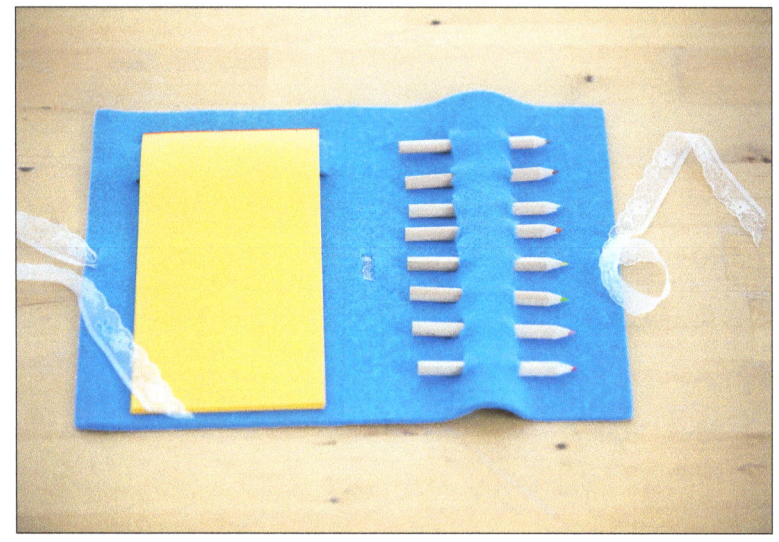

How to make:

1. Use the 'stationary wrap' template on page 77 as a guide. Use a ruler and chalk to mark all the dashes onto the felt sheet.
2. Use the craft knife to create slits by cutting along the dashes.
3. Place pencils and pad in their slots.
4. Thread ribbon through the ribbon holes.

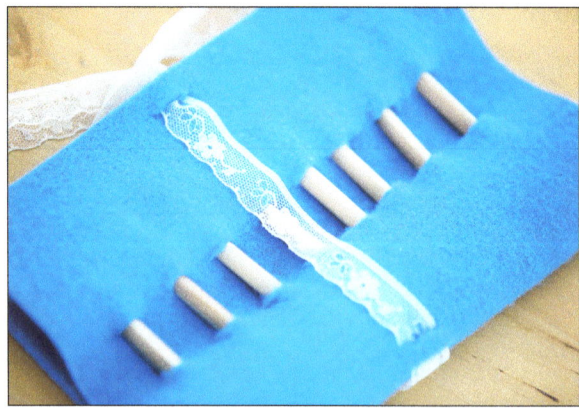

47. Pencil Wrap

Make this for yourself or a friend! It's also an awesome way to display your pencils. Roll it up and enjoy!

Things you need:

- 21 x 29.7 cm (A4) felt sheet
- 30 cm ribbon
- Tailor's chalk
- Needle
- Thread
- Craft knife
- Craft Mat
- Ruler

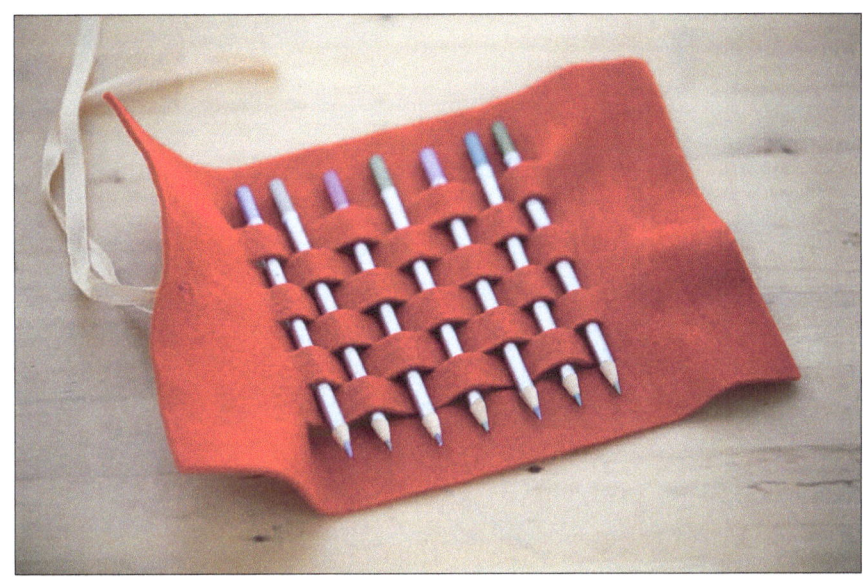

How to make:

1. Use the 'pencil wrap' template on page 77 as a guide. Use a ruler and chalk to mark all the lines onto the felt sheet.
2. Use the craft knife to create 7 slits by cutting along the lines.
3. Hand sew the middle of the ribbon on the reverse side of the 'x' marking. This will be used to tie the wrap together.
4. Place pencils in their slots and roll the sheet, then tie the ribbon.

Templates

-------- = Fold   _____ = Cut

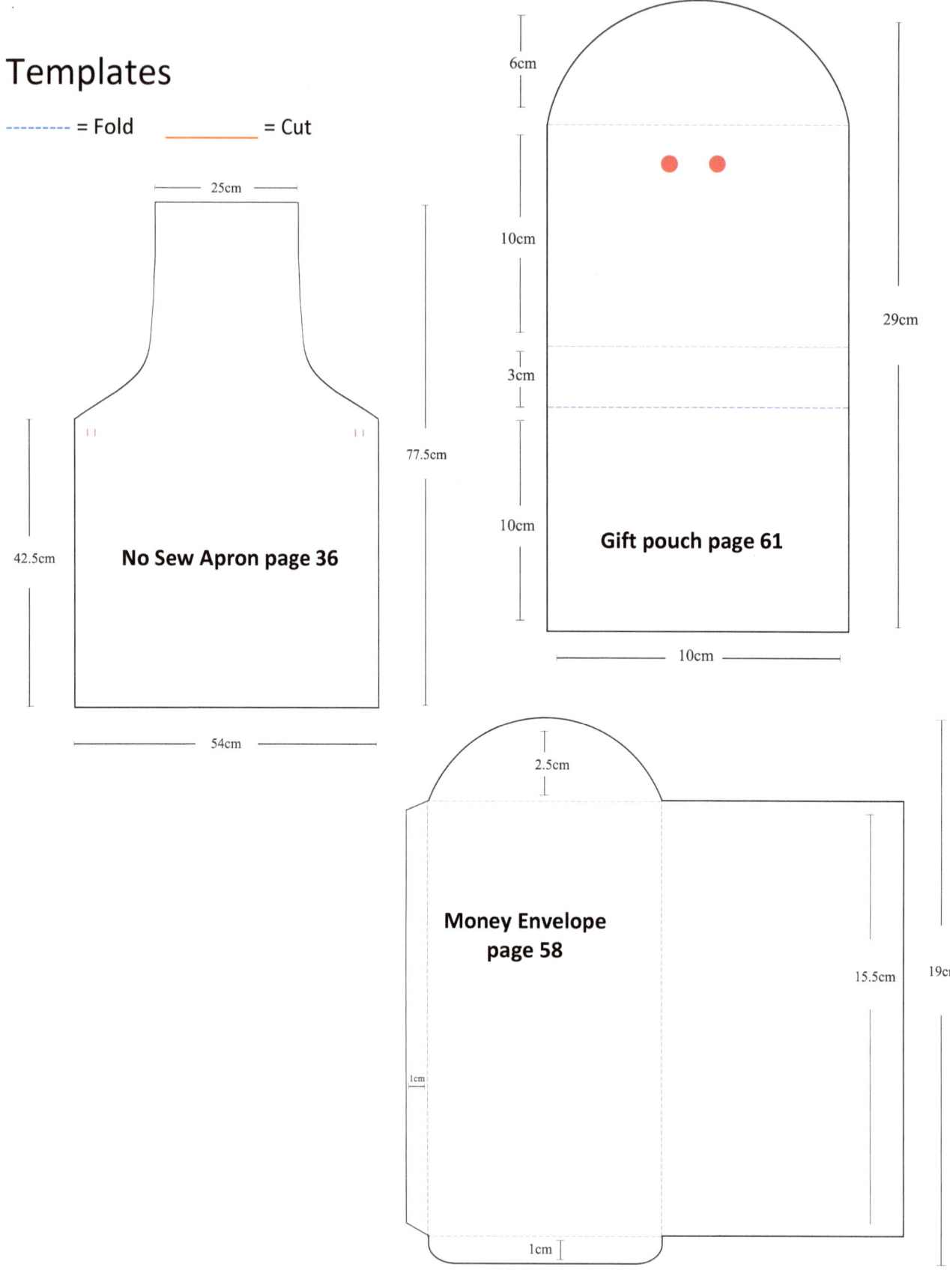

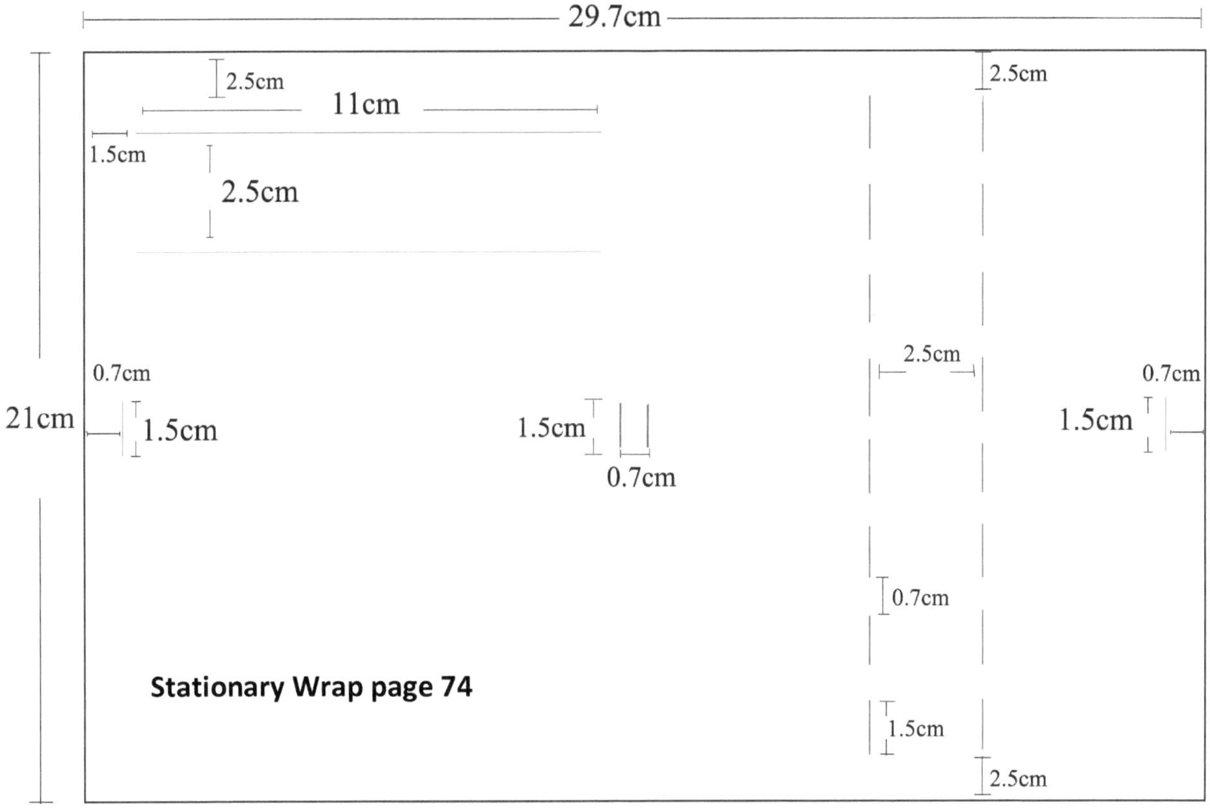
29.7cm
2.5cm
11cm
1.5cm
2.5cm
2.5cm
21cm
0.7cm
1.5cm
1.5cm
0.7cm
2.5cm
0.7cm
1.5cm
0.7cm
1.5cm
2.5cm
Stationary Wrap page 74

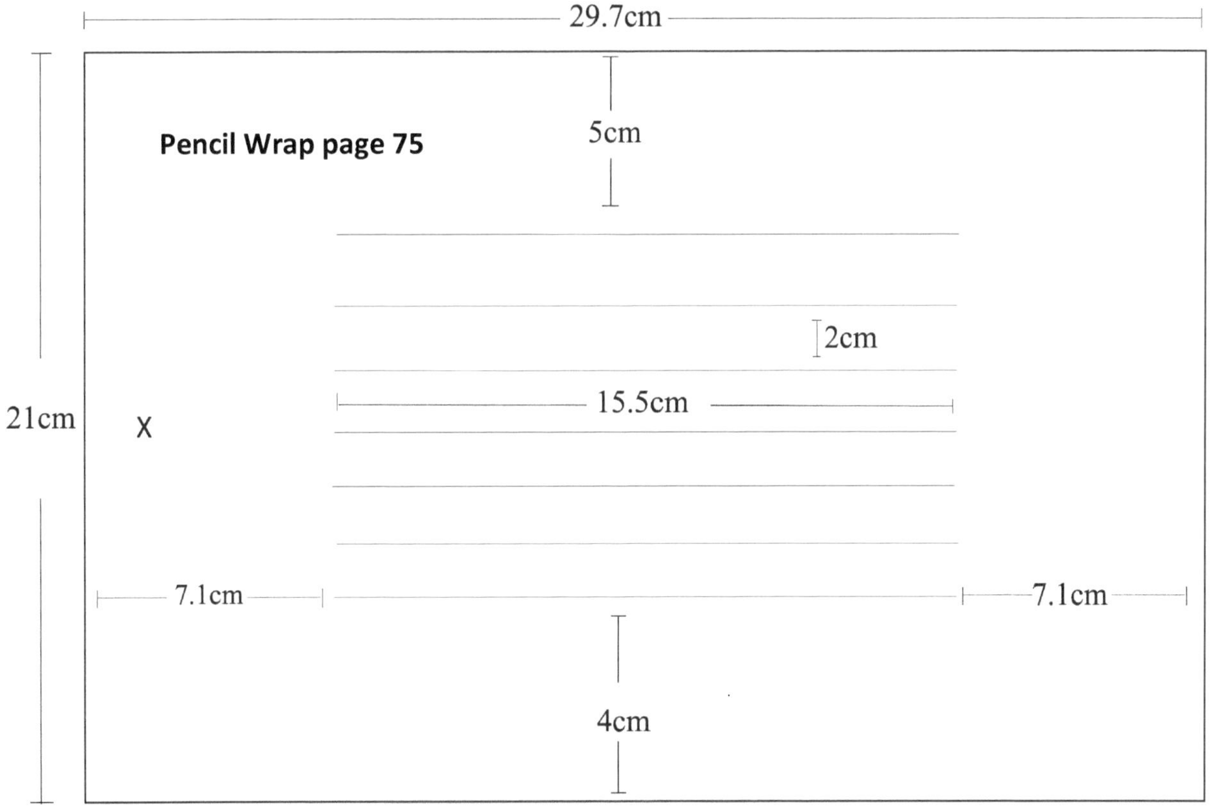
29.7cm
Pencil Wrap page 75
5cm
2cm
15.5cm
21cm
X
7.1cm
7.1cm
4cm

Good Deeds Activity List

1. Smile at a stranger.
2. Wake your family up for Fajr prayer.
3. Hold a door open for someone.
4. Be grateful for what you have and do not envy others.
5. Make dua for your parents; "Rabbir ham-humaa kamaa rabbayaani sagheera", 'My Lord, bestow upon them your Mercy as they did bring me up when I was young.' (Al Israa; 24).
6. Help your siblings with homework
7. Never mock or backbite anyone.
8. Donate your Islamic books to other children.
9. Try you best to pray all 5 prayers on time.
10. Thank Allah and remember him as much as you can.
11. Give dates to your neighbour and friends to break fast.
12. Make a phone call to your family just to say, 'Salam' and check how they're doing.
13. Invite friends to have iftar at your house.
14. Read Qur'an and teach it to your siblings.
15. Make a list of things that you're thankful for and say Alhamdulillah.
16. Sell your things online and give the proceeds to charity.
17. Help your parents make iftar.
18. Pick up rubbish on the street and throw it in the bin.
19. Help with the household chores.
20. Recycle items and don't waste things.
21. Be patient and avoid getting angry.
22. Make an Eid gift for your teacher.
23. If there is any leftover iftar, give it away.
24. Say nice things or keep quiet.
25. Always have good manners.

Glossary

Alhamdulillah: All Praise is to Allah (swt).

Allah: Arabic name for God.

AS: A'layhi Salam – Peace be upon him.

Ayah: Verse from the Qur'an.

Dua: Supplication.

Dhikr: Remembrance of Allah (swt)

Eid al Fitr: Festival of break fast.

Eid al Adha: Festival of the sacrifice.

Iftar: The evening meal that breaks the daily fast in Ramadan.

Iftar Dua: Zahabadh-dhama'u wabtallatil-'urooqu, wa thabatal-ajru inshaa-Allaahu - The thirst has gone and the veins are quenched, and reward is confirmed, if Allah (swt) wills. (Abu Dawud)

Jannah: Paradise.

Muslim: A person who follows and believes in the religion of Islam.

Prophet Muhammad (pbuh): The final prophet sent to mankind.

PBUH: Peace be upon him.

Ramadan: The ninth month of the Islamic year.

Sadaqah: Voluntary charity.

Salah: Prayer.

Suhoor: The pre dawn meal eaten by Muslims in Ramadan.

Sunnah: Ways, deeds and acts of the Prophet Muhammad (pbuh).

Surah: A chapter in the Qur'an.

SWT: Subhana Wa Ta'ala – The Most Glorified, the Most High, referring only to Allah (swt).

Qur'an: The book from Allah (swt) revealed to the Prophet Muhammad (pbuh) through the Angel Jibreel (as).

Zakat: One of the five pillars of Islam where obligatory charity must be given by Muslims (who meet the requirement).

www.ingramcontent.com/pod-product-compliance
Lightning Source LLC
Chambersburg PA
CBHW041159290426
44109CB00002B/63